Encounters

with

Animals

Barbara Linder

Encounters

with

Animals

Table of Contents

Introduction

But ask the animals and they will teach you; the birds of the air and they will tell you...in [God's] hand is the life of every living thing and the breath of every human being.

—Job 12:7,10

I have always loved animals, large and small, and have never been afraid of any I have encountered. I am saddened by the many species facing extinction due to loss of habitat, pesticides, and global warming. A new understanding of the relationship between humans and animals is emerging and is much needed. That relationship is a major focus of this book.

Aristotle, an ancient Greek philosopher, is considered one of the greatest intellectual figures in Western history. His concepts remain embedded in Western thinking to this day. He argued that all life could be ranked from "lower" to "higher," with humans at the top. During the Middle Ages, Christian theologians adopted Aristotle's idea and talked about a great chain of being. When our nation was founded, only white men who owned land could vote. Hierarchical thinking persists and has led to the misuse and abuse of the poor, persons of color, women, and animals.

Moreover, because of the long-standing focus on sin and redemption, Christians have neglected God's desire for us to be in loving relationship with Him, with our neighbors near and far, and with animals as fellow creatures. That is an important part of the opening chapters of the Bible and a thread that moves through subsequent chapters.

In the chapters that follow, the focus is on nine of the animals with which I have had encounters: dogs, snakes, squirrels, spiders, bears, eagles, song birds, elk, and monarch butterflies. I share what I have experienced and learned from those encounters, what the animal has symbolized in some cultures, and what we can all learn from those animals. In the epilogue, I offer some suggestions for co-existing with compassion with our fellow creatures.

I encourage you to read one chapter at a time, reflecting on the questions at the close of each chapter. If you are a person who journals, I encourage you to do that with the questions. I also encourage you to spend some time outside— whether on your porch or patio, in the back yard, at a nearby park, or on a hiking trail. Take time to sit in silence, quietly listening and seeing, and so becoming aware of the animals above, below, and all around you.

Chapter 1

It's All about Relationships

Look at the birds of the air; they neither sow or reap, nor gather into barns, and yet your heavenly Father feeds them.

Matthew 6:26

For thousands of years, people have pondered the meaning of life. Why am I here? What is my purpose? What will give me happiness? Where do I find fulfillment? Finding satisfactory answers to these important questions is important for personal development in our formative years. We may face them again after retiring from a challenging career, when facing an empty nest, or after experiencing a personal tragedy.

I first faced these questions as a teenager. There were also questions about God. Does God really care about me? If God is in charge, why is there so much evil in the world? Why doesn't being a person of faith give one the courage to do the right thing when it is unpopular?

I am thankful for my pastor at that time, who welcomed my questions and shared that there were no easy answers. When I was in ninth grade, he told me it was important for me to grow spiritually as I grew intellectually. He proposed that I read the Bible from cover to cover and that we would discuss it together. His gift made a significant difference in my life and in my career choice.

Built into the human makeup is a longing, a restlessness, for more than everyday experiences. The answer to that search can finally be found only in faith in a loving God. The mystic Thomas Merton famously wrote, "Ultimately, faith is the only key to the universe. The final meaning of human existence and the answers on which all happiness depends cannot be found in any other way."[1]

The first question I raised with my pastor was "Why are there two creation stories in the opening chapters of Genesis?" He helped me to learn to take the Bible very seriously without taking it literally. Those Genesis accounts are not history like we read in history books. They are not scientific facts. They are myths that speak to a deeper truth than scientific facts. They are stories that reach an important place in our hearts and minds. The naturalist Lyanda Lynn Haupt puts the various ways of knowing this way:

> As perilous and complex as these times are, we are armed with a rare trio of tools that offer a rooted way forward: the joining of nature, spirit, and a uniquely modern science. The innate connection between humans and the natural

world is coming to fore in a new way, as academic research rises in support of truths that poets, writers, mystics, artists, naturalists, earth-based religions, and Indigenous cultures have always proclaimed.[2]

The Genesis stories tell the truth about God and God's desire for humankind and the rest of creation. Ponder this: God did not have to create heaven and earth. The triune God was already in relationship—three in one and one in three. That is a closer relationship than we can ever experience. A myriad of angels surrounds God. Yet somehow, God wanted more.

God's love is so overflowing that God wanted to be in relationship with you and with me. Simply put, creation is an act of divine love. God wants to be in a loving relationship with us and wants to be in a loving relationship with others, including animals. We are created in a way for these relationships to flourish; however, we must make the efforts needed. That's why the coronavirus epidemic has been so hard. That's why our hearts are restless until we respond in faith and love.

In Genesis 2:19, we read that God gave Adam the responsibility of naming "every living creature." We miss the point if we think there is no way he named every animal from the aardvark to the zebra. So why is that verse there? Why the story of the naming of the animals? Think of what is behind the naming of newborn children. Many are named for family members from past generations. Naming is an act of relationship. It says the child is a member of an extended family.

We human animals are called by God to be in relationship with other animals—and not just our pet companions. Richard Louv, in his great book titled *Our Wild Calling,* notes, "Each animal we encounter has the potential to become part of us or part of who we could become. If we meet them halfway."[3] Jenny Leading Cloud of the White River Sioux put it this way:

> The buffalo and the coyote are our brothers, the birds our cousins. Even the tiniest ant, even a louse, even the smallest flower you can find—they are all our relatives. We end our prayers with the words *mitakuye oyasin*—"all my relations"—and that all includes everything that grows, crawls, runs, creeps, hops and flies on this continent.[4]

Saint Francis of Assisi (1181-1226) is known for his love of animals. He called them "brothers" and "sisters." In his famous "Canticle of the Creatures" he wrote, "You are glorified, O God, in all your creatures."[5] Like many congregations across the country, the ones I served had a blessing of the animals around October 4, the feast day for Francis. Animals and their guardians gathered in a large circle in the yard. There was always a variety of animals, but the majority were usually dogs.

As I knelt and put my hands on their heads, we looked at each other eye-to-eye. It seemed soul-to-soul—as if they knew I was asking God to bless them. I hold those experiences deep in my heart. But the most memorable one was a calf. The morning of the blessing, a dairy farmer asked if she could bring the calf. The calf's anxious behavior was causing havoc among the herd.

The husband brought the calf in a trailer that evening. The calf was the last to receive a blessing. I placed my hands on the calf's head, and talked to it and prayed, looking eye-to-eye. The next morning the dairy farmer called and said amazingly all was well in the barn. She asked, "What did you do?"

As I explained to her, I have no special powers. However, I trust that God's loving touch can flow though our hands to bring peace and healing. We need only to offer up ourselves to be a conduit. It is God's Spirit touching our spirit. I also trust that there is a deeper, more mysterious relationship between humans and animals than most of us realize.

Too often, animals are simply seen as our pets, as domestic workers, food for families, or wildly threatening. Animals are killed for sport, for their parts, or in scientific experimentation. What if we saw animals that soar through the skies, that swim the oceans deep, that walk through forests and plains, that creep, crawl, and cavort on our lawns, as family? What if we took the time to learn just how amazing animals are?

Louv shares the experience that Jay Griffths of Wales had. Griffiths once spent hours watching ants in his garden. A small piece of apple had fallen to the ground. He watched as one, then two, then finally enough ants arrived. According to Griffiths,

"They did, together, begin to move it, and the episode became a strangely intense time, as I realized that in the nature of deep concentration, I had lost track of time, but also that I had lost track of scale. After some time, I suddenly looked up, and my garden (a tiny plot of land) looked like a massive and endless forest." [6]

Suspension of time, and even a shift in scale, can happen amid our encounters with animals. We can learn things about and from our animal brothers and sisters. Just think how much better those tiny ants worked together than our representatives in Washington do today. Suspension of time and shift of scale can also lead to spiritual growth.

For Reflection:

1. Are there animals you are afraid of? Why?

2. Are there animals you have formed a close bond with? How was that bond created? How did it change you?

3. Do you agree that God's creation is an act of love? Why or why not?

4. Do you feel superior to animals? If so, in what ways?

5. Have you ever participated in a blessing of animals? If so, what was the experience like for you and your animal companion?

6. What would it mean for the world if everyone thought of animals as our companions, our relatives?

Chapter 2

Dogs

It takes a lot to break a dog's spirit. Its ability to love, even when abused, is tremendous. Its spirit and willingness to love and be a companion is great.[7]

The above quotation from Ted Andrews speaks to the dog companions I have had. But first let us consider dogs in general. Some time ago, in the distant past, dogs evolved from wolves. Dogs first appear to be domesticated some 15,000 years ago. Dogs and humans have shared environments for thousands of years.

In ancient Greece, a dog was a companion to the dying and the guardian of the dead. The Roman philosopher Cicero thought dogs were capable of expressing gratitude, which he considered to be the highest virtue. In early Christianity the dog "was a symbol of guardianship...and even an allegory for the priest," according to Andrews.[8]

Most Native Americans had dogs for protection. Today, Americans have dogs for a variety of reasons. For many homeless in our cities and towns, a dog is both protection and companionship. There are therapy dogs, rescue dogs, and dogs who visit schools, hospitals, and nursing homes. For many of us, they are beloved companions.

Using dogs as a part of therapy goes back to the late eighteenth century when dogs were introduced into mental institutions to help socialize patients. Service dogs are now trained to detect and act on behaviors associated with PTSD and with particular positions on the autism spectrum. One study found that seniors with dogs improved their walking capacities 28 percent in twelve weeks.[9]

Louv cites a 2017 review of existing research which found evidence of an association with pet companionship and a wide range of benefits including increased self-esteem and social competence, decreased loneliness, wider social networks, and even cognitive benefits. He notes, "When we take good care of a dog, it takes good care of us: it protects us, and our interactions with it lowers our blood pressure and improves our mental health. We become each other in that sense."[10] Is it any wonder that so many of us love dogs?

There are about one billion dogs around the world today. Sadly, only one-fourth of them are companion animals. The rest are strays who scavenge for food. It is estimated that thirteen to sixteen million dogs are killed and consumed in Asia every year, where eating dog meat goes back to antiquity. Dogs are still used in scientific experiments in the United States, causing them pain and death.

My first relationship with a dog started when I was five years old. A neighbor up the block had a large boxer that many were afraid of simply because it was so big. I don't remember how it started, but that boxer and I became buddies. I rode it like a pony up and down the block. The boxer looked for me and when it saw me it knelt down so I could get on. That boxer taught me early on that when we show no fear and no aggression, then animals can be great companions.

I did not have a dog companion of my own until I was past graduate school and working at a university. He was a beagle pup named Blue. Friends who raised beagles as a hobby gave me the runt of the litter. Blue did not live long before his heart gave out due to a defect. A surgeon asked if he could do an autopsy and so learn more since some human infants have similar heart defects.

My friends and I grieved Blue's passing, but we were glad that in death he might have helped an infant live.

For several reasons, including my busy schedule, I did not get another dog for several years. I was serving an exurban congregation and the church secretary knew I loved dogs. One day, she called and invited me to come to her house to meet Spike. He was a two year-old Samoyed who had run away from the fourth man who had had him in his short life; the man was not interested in getting Spike back.

Spike came right to me. Still, it took some time to bond. He acted like a therapy dog when parishioners came to talk with me. Spike went to them and as they petted him with his thick, soft fur, they relaxed and then told me what was bothering them. In a sense, Spike was a wounded healer.

Walking a sixty-pound plus dog kept me in shape. He came with me when I retired and loved romping in the fenced back yard, chasing rabbits and squirrels. The first time I took him in the car he cried like a baby, afraid that I was abandoning him as others had. But by our long trip from Minnesota to Colorado, he knew that would never happen. In many ways, Spike was my closest dog companion and it was really hard to say good bye the day his body gave out.

I trust that someday I will see Spike again. I am certainly not alone in the hope that we will be reunited in the life to come with the animals we so deeply loved. After meeting with a little boy who was grieving for a dog who had died, Pope Francis reportedly said, "One day, we will see our animals again in the eternity of Christ."[11] I agree with Francis that no creature is forgotten in God's sight. It is just how a God of amazing love responds.

My life with Spike convinced me that all my future dog companions would come from shelters or humane societies. That's where I found Max, a seven-year-old Springer spaniel. He had clearly been abused and then abandoned. He soon showed he was a real lover. We bonded quickly, but it took longer for him to be comfortable with everyone who visited. It also took time for him to walk at my speed.

One day, as we were on our morning walk, two pit bulls came running toward us. Max was afraid and got behind me. No guard dog was he! I am thankful those two dogs obeyed my command to *"Stay!"* Finally their guardian came and apologized. I still gave him a piece of my mind. We need to take good care of our dog companions, and that includes being responsible guardians.

The average dog can understand and respond to nearly 300 human words. With specialized training, they understand even more. My dog companions have also shown me they sense our moods. When a group of friends visited, Max, like Spike, seemed to know who needed some time with him.

The day Max died was another sad one. I was appreciative of friends who were there for me. After some time of grieving, I brought my first female dog home from the local humane society. Bee is a mix of Labrador retriever and border collie, and was six years old when she came to live with me. She was another abused and neglected dog who had been left out morning, noon, and night regardless of the weather. It took a long time to really bond. She is still terrified of thunderstorms and remains more comfortable with women than men.

Sometimes Bee looks at me with her soulful eyes as if she is expressing gratitude. Dogs are not meant to be alone any more than we are. God created us to be in relationship. During the isolation brought on by the pandemic, I have been often thankful for Bee's companionship. People write about a pandemic of loneliness in our country. One way to relieve that loneliness is to get a dog as a companion. I encourage you to get one from a shelter. As one of my t-shirts puts it: "Second hand dogs make first class pets".

For Reflection:

1. Why can our wounds make us better healers?
2. A friend likes to remind me that "dog" is "God" spelled backwards. What does that suggest to you?
3. What does it mean to you that the relationship between humans and dogs is 15,000 years long?
4. If you have had an animal companion, what did that relationship teach you?
5. If you are able, visit an area shelter and learn about their needs. What would it mean if more people got their pets from shelters?

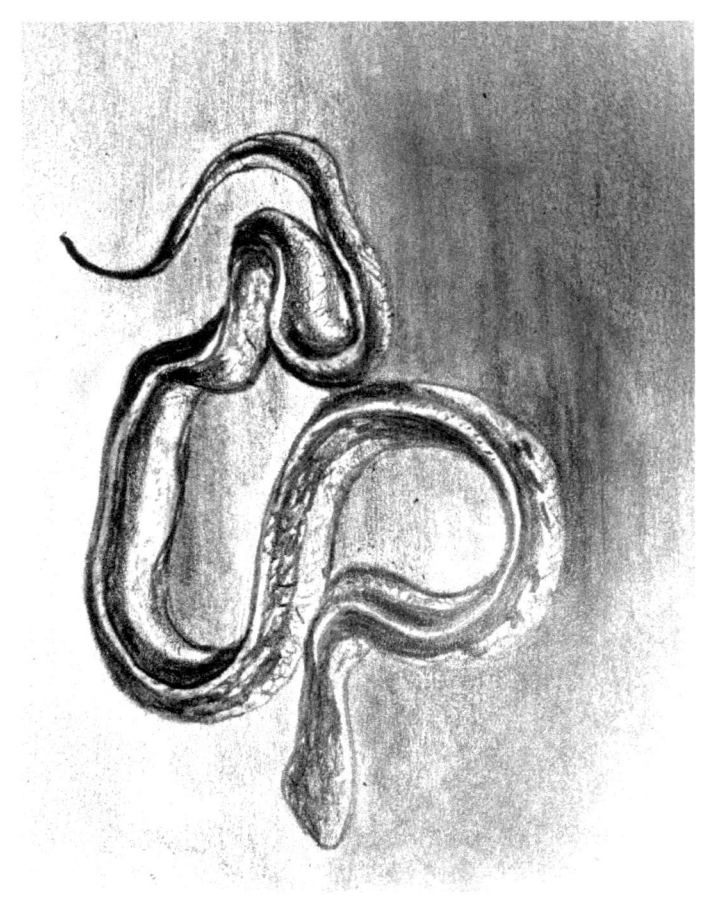

Chapter 3

Snakes

There is another way of seeing that involves letting go. When I see this way, I sway transfixed and emptied.[12]

Annie Dillard

There are more than 30,000 species of snakes found around the world, except in Greenland, Iceland, New Zealand, and Antarctica. Only 20 percent of the species is venomous; of these poisonous snakes, only seven percent are able to kill or significantly wound a person. That means the common fear of snakes is overblown.

Still, according to the World Health Organization, as many as 138,000 people die from snake bites annually. Sadly, almost all of these deaths occur in poor, rural communities in developing countries. Reasons for this include a shortage of anti-venoms (the only medicine that can neutralize the deadly toxins and which must be kept refrigerated), lack of money or transportation, lack of staff training, and distrust of Western medicine.

Many have a fear or distaste for snakes. In Genesis 3:1, we are told that "the serpent was craftier than any other of the wild animals that the Lord God made." Many think the serpent was a snake. In the story, the serpent is a metaphor for anything in creation that can tempt humans and so seduce them away from God.

But the snake is also a healer, in both symbol and fact. For the Native Americans, the snake is a symbol of healing and transformation. In ancient Greece, the snake was also a symbol for healing. The Greek god Hermes carried a staff upon which were entwined two snakes. This symbolic staff became the primary symbol of modern medicine and doctors. As Andrews puts it, "It is a symbol of wisdom expressed though healing."[13]

The venom from poisonous snakes has highly developed proteins which have curative powers. It is known to have cured some cancers, and a drug made from the venom reduces blood clotting. So, we might say that snakes are a subject filled with paradox.

My first encounter with snakes came when I was four or five years of age. The kids in the neighborhood played in the woods across from our home. The rite of passage was to pick up one of the many garter snakes crawling around in the woods. To show the kids how brave I was I picked up two snakes—one in each hand. When I ran across the road to show my mom, she was so frightened she locked me out of the house.

Garter snakes are harmless. When I have seen one in my garden over the years, I have welcomed it. Garter snakes eat critters that can do damage to vegetables and flowers. On the other hand, while hiking Colorado trails, with signs warning of rattlesnakes in the area, I am careful. I have never encountered a rattlesnake and do not care to meet one up close.

Because it sheds its skin, the snake has been a symbol of death and rebirth for a long time. Before it sheds its skin, its eyes get cloudy, as if it is entering a stage between life and death. The rebirth symbolized includes seeing ourselves and the world anew.

There are many areas of life that may need death and rebirth. As I have reflected on my behavior in the woods that day so long ago, I see it as an early example of how competitive I was. I loved winning. I loved being the best.

I saw more clearly how much that was a part of me when I attended a continuing education workshop on the Enneagram. The roots of the Enneagram go back many centuries, and it was rediscovered in our country in the 1960s. The Enneagram models nine personality types that explain why we behave as we do. All nine types are needed for balance in companies and organizations. Competitiveness is part of my type eight personality.

Competition can be good or bad. Teams improve when they face strong competition. Competition engages the mind to improvise and improve things. Winning can give a person a needed dose of self-esteem, a sense of self-worth. Our economic system is built on competition. In an informative and timely book on the need for antitrust legislation, Senator Amy Klobuchar writes:

> When a corporation transforms itself from a competition to a monopolist, it wields considerable power—power over wages, power over markets and power over the economy itself. Thriving competitive companies are essential to our economy and to the American way of life.[14]

So, competition can be beneficial in some ways, but it is harmful in other ways. Competition leads to making comparisons. If I am the winner, you are a loser—of a match, a promotion, or an election. If I am right, then you are wrong. There is no room for compromise for the common good.

This zero-sum thinking undermines relationships and hinders personal growth. It is a source of the ills in our country today. Keeping the focus on ourselves rather than working with others and building them up is detrimental in many ways; it erodes the bonds of society and undermines our democracy.

Some people try to hide that they are competitive. That seems to be especially true of women who think they should not be competitive—that it is not ladylike to be so. This is really a form of passive aggressiveness that can come out at home or at the office or at church.

Competition became less of an issue for me as I matured. I saw how it could undermine relationships. Through meditation and prayer, I saw how my competitiveness was tied to perfectionism and workaholism. I am grateful to be at a point of self-acceptance and acceptance of others. I have been able to slow down what drove me. It is still more fun to win at games, but my self-image is not affected when I lose.

One day Jesus told his followers, "Those who want to save their life will lose it and those who lose their life for my sake and for the sake of the gospel will save it" (Mark 9:35). I think Jesus was talking about far more than the martyrdom that was in the future for some of them. If we focus only on ourselves, we lose out on so much that makes life meaningful, fulfilling, hopeful, and joyous.

Like a snake sheds its skin, we need to shed all that keeps us from a life of love. The gospel proclaims God's love for all of us, and Jesus challenges us to love God, ourselves, and others in return. A life of such love is a new birth indeed.

For Reflection:

1. What is your attitude toward snakes? Why?
2. Do you have a competitive spirit? How has it affected your relationships with others?
3. Are there areas of your life that need death and rebirth?
4. Are there behaviors or practices that you need to shed?
5. Is it true, as the saying goes, what doesn't kill you makes you stronger?

Chapter 4

Squirrels

The squirrel does not live by nuts alone.
It obviously enjoys life,
And even has an antic sense of humor.[15]

A.B.C. Whipple

When I was in second grade, we moved to what my parents called "a better neighborhood." That meant a new school, a new teacher, and making new friends in the middle of the year. I missed my old school and my old friends and playing in the woods. At least there was a large tree in our back yard that waited to be climbed.

One day after school, I encountered what would become an unexpected buddy. I saw a squirrel that had been mauled, likely by a hawk or an owl. The squirrel lay listlessly on the ground. I went inside to get some salve, peanuts, and a small bowl of water. I carefully picked up the squirrel and put it on my lap. It let me tend to its wounds and then ate a few peanuts and went to sleep on my lap.

As a child, I did not know that squirrels can carry rabies. I would not have picked it up with my bare hands if I had known. But I certainly would not have left it to die. The squirrel slowly healed and its vitality returned. Every afternoon, it looked for me and then leaped onto my lap. Even when it was completely healed, it continued that behavior for some time. Finally, one day it paired off with another squirrel who visited. Later, I sometimes saw the two of them cavorting on the tree limbs.

It is amazing to think that a small creature could show seeming gratitude and friendship. That squirrel was the closest thing to a pet I had while living with my parents. For me, it is just an example of the relationship God intends us to have with animals. We are called to be the guardians of the small ones we see in our yards and may have in our homes.

Squirrels are small creatures that many see in yards and parks. If you feed birds, you may have battled them as you tried to find a squirrel-proof feeder. I discovered a place they couldn't reach but I could watch the birds. The squirrels just fed on the seeds the birds dropped.

I have had many chuckles watching the squirrels tease my dogs. They know just how high the dog can leap and then stay just out of the dog's reach. They keep chirping at the dog, who sometimes barks back until one or the other gets tired of playing.

Squirrels are the most numerous of mammals. They are members of the rodent family, which ranges from mice to beavers. Red squirrels are most commonly found in woods and forests. Grey squirrels are most commonly found in cities and suburbs. The fur of the grey squirrel is tan with shades of black and a white underside. So-called flying squirrels do not really fly; their skin stretches and so enables them to glide from tree to tree.

The most remarkable part of a squirrel is its tail. It is half the length of its body and serves like a rudder when the squirrel is jumping from tree to tree. In winter, when the squirrel curls up in its nest, the tail functions as a blanket. On a rainy day, it serves as an umbrella.

Many of us have enjoyed seeing squirrels frolicking and making death-defying leaps from tree to tree. Whipple shares those squirrels made a contribution to early American history. In his words,

> The squirrel was one of the most difficult targets for early marksmen, not only because it could flatten itself against a tree to become nearly invisible. As a result,

early American squirrel hunters became the best sharpshooters in the world. And during the American Revolution it was the minuteman with his squirrel rifle who picked off, one by one, the British soldiers trained to advance in ranks. .[16]

The British should have learned from the squirrels!

During the summer months, squirrels can be seen digging holes in the ground to store food. If another squirrel is watching, the squirrel may pretend to put the nut in the ground but keeps it in its mouth. They may forget where they hid their caches, but their keen sense of smell helps them to find those caches even if they have forgotten where they stored their food for winter.

So, what can the squirrel teach us? There are two related things: learn to ration and save for later, and take time to socialize and play. What makes them related is the issue of materialism lying underneath. Materialism suggests that individuals work as hard as they can to make as much as they can so they have enough to live well. That is the lifestyle promoted by the advertisers and media.

My goal for managing my income is 80-10-10. This means spending 80 percent of income on self, including household, vehicle, and travel. Save 10 percent for unexpected and future expenses, and donate 10 percent to organizations and causes I care about. I do not reach that goal sometimes. But it keeps me asking myself. *Do you really need that?* It stops impulse buying. It involves making a budget and keeping to it the best I can.

Such money management is not easy, but it is worth the effort. One is satisfied with enough rather than always striving for more, or for the latest. One is grateful rather than grabbing. Like squirrels hide nuts for the lean months, so we save for unexpected emergencies.

The hardest part for me is not management of money but taking time to socialize and play. My workaholism, and its unhealthy twin perfectionism, began at an early age. Nothing less than an A was expected by my parents and teachers. It was also the way to earn the scholarship that enabled me to go to college. Most of my decades as a university administrator, professor, and parish pastor involved far more than forty-hour work weeks. There was always more to do than time to do it.

I am not alone in this. Many workers today do not even take the vacation time offered them. American workers work longer hours than their European counterparts. The focus is on what we do for a living rather than who we are as people. Some retired folks have calendars as full as when they were working. I even remember an older man in a suit carrying his briefcase to read the newspaper in the nursing home where he lived.

In my retirement, I keep busy but have learned to say no to some requests for my time. I enjoy dinners, road trips, and walks with friends.

Book clubs, walks with Bee, and playing dominoes are on my schedule. There are also jigsaw puzzles and a magazine of Sudoku puzzles at hand. For most of my life, I have read at least one book a week.

What does play time look like for you? Play makes life more enjoyable. Friends who volunteer together and who play together deepen their friendships. God commanded us to keep the Sabbath. Most of the time, we think of Sabbath time as going to church or synagogue. But Sabbath time is rest time. Genesis tells us God rested on the seventh day. Play is related to rest in the sense that it gets our mind off of work and other issues we are wrestling with. Play can be the prelude to rest that satisfies and renews, that helps us see in new ways.

One Sabbath, when Jesus was criticized by some religious leaders for being neglectful of one of the many laws, they had promulgated for keeping the Sabbath, he said to them, "The

Sabbath is made for humankind and not humankind for the Sabbath" (Mark 2:27).

Sabbath time is a gift to be used. Take time to play and to pray. Go outside and walk barefoot on the grass, feeling and listening and seeing the sights and sounds of nature around you. You may be pleasantly surprised.

For Reflection:

1. What do you think of squirrels?
2. Have you ever had an unexpected buddy in the animal world?
3. How does the message of buy, buy, buy affect you?
4. Is it difficult for you to take time to play? To pray? Why?
5. What is enjoyable play for you?

Chapter 5

Spiders

Oh, what a tangled web we weave,
When first we practice to deceive![17]

Sir Walter Scott

A lot of people fear, or have an aversion to, spiders. But like most animals, there is more to spiders than meets the eye. Of the more than 46,700 species of spiders, only a few species are toxic to humans, most notably the black widow and brown recluse. Spiders range in body length from very small to the very big, hairy tarantula.

Spiders are not insects. They have eight legs, not six. They are in the class called *arachnoids*. The name comes from Ariadne, a talented weaver who, according to Greek mythology, issued a challenge to Athena, the Greek goddess of wisdom and war. Ariadne claimed she was a better weaver than Athena. The punishment for her arrogance was that she was turned into a spider.

All spiders are predators, feeding mostly on insects. They eat between 400-800 billion pounds of insects each year. Anne Sverdrup-Thygeson notes, "That's more than the entire human population manages to polish off even if we combine meat and fish."[18]

Spiders have been used to control insects in Israeli apple orchards and Chinese rice fields. Large numbers have also been found in American fields. We should remember those benefits of spiders when we are tempted to kill one.

Some spiders chase and overpower their prey. More species weave silk webs as snares to trap prey. On a per weight basis, spider silk is six times stronger than steel. Even though it is so strong it is elastic; it gives some so the web can trap flying insects.

One morning, as I was trying to write a sermon, I got stuck. The biblical text for the coming Sunday dealt with Jesus's call to forgive others. I could not decide how to deal with it. So I took a break.

I looked out the window. A spider came down from somewhere above the window on a filament of silk, launched itself to a branch on an azalea bush and then started making a large intricate web as the silk came out of its body. I was enthralled as I watched this beautiful creation.

Suddenly, I heard an inner voice say, "Forgive your brother as I have forgiven you." That brother is five years younger than me. We had a rocky relationship for years. I had been hurt and frustrated by some of his behaviors. My prayer was basically, "God, shape him up!" But God had other plans. I shared my morning experience in my sermon, including a commitment to work on forgiving my brother. I am thankful that, with work on both our parts, we are now in a much better place. Webster's dictionary defines a web as "something by which one is entangled, involved in difficulties, held fast, or impeded in one's progress." The failure to forgive left both of us in a web that we had to break out of.

Forgiveness is never easy. It is not the same thing as forgetting. Indeed, that difference is important for victims of child or sexual abuse. Forgiveness is a matter of heart and head. It is recognizing the reality that sometimes we misunderstand or don't know the whole story behind someone's actions when we are hurt by them. Forgiveness takes listening with love. Forgiveness frees us from the web of distrust and hurt we feel. It makes restored relationships possible.

I am always amazed by the stories of people who quickly forgive those who murdered their family members or friends—from Amish parents of schoolchildren to members of a Bible study at an historic Black church. I wonder how easy it really is for them. I think two things may be involved. First, they know that harboring bitterness and revenge would only prolong their pain and suffering. Second, as people of faith, they lived out Jesus's call to "love your enemies and pray for those who persecute you" (Matthew 6:44). Sometimes, such acts of forgiveness transform murderers, even when they don't give peace to those who forgive.

As Soren Kierkegaard wrote, "The only true forgiveness is that which is offered and extended even before the offender has apologized and sought it." Another writer of that time noted, "Forgiveness is man's deepest need and highest achievement."[19]

That quotation by Horace Bushell reminds us that we all need forgiveness for the things we have done and left undone. We all have hurt others by our actions and inaction, whether intentionally or not.

Many parishioners over the years have asked me, "How can I forgive ____?" Forgiveness is not easy. It is not natural. It is not our first response. Some crimes against humanity seem unforgiveable. Anger, moral indignation, rage, or flight is our first response.

Forgiveness from the head and heart is a discipline that one must practice over and over again, all the time remembering that we are so commanded by the One who loves us in spite of all our faults and failures. Forgiveness is not easy. "To err is human, to forgive divine," wrote Alexander Pope, coining a cliché. Forgiveness is joyful; reconciling and forgiveness is required.

In many Native American traditions, the spider is both grandmother and creator. Andrews writes that "it is the symbol of the ability to weave new energies into being."[20] That is a reminder that the web can also be a positive symbol. It is the symbol of the interconnectedness of all of us and with all creation. It is an important symbol to keep in front of us during the critical time in which we live.

The fourteenth-century mystic, Julian of Norwich, penned a book of her meditations. One goes this way:

> We are all created at the same time;
>
> and in our creation we are knit and one to God.
>
> By this we are kept luminous and noble
>
> as when we were created.
>
> By the force of this precious one being
>
> we love, seek, praise, thank
>
> and endlessly enjoy our Creator.[21]

As one, may we weave new energies of love, of forgiveness, and of restoration of relationships as God intends.

For Reflection:

1. Is there someone you need to forgive for your own well-being?

2. Are you caught in some kind of web? What would it take to get free?

3. In what ways are you connected to and with others?

4. Right now in our country, it seems that scoring points is more important than understanding others. What would it take to turn things around?

Chapter 6

Bears

When all is said and done, doesn't coexisting with bears
really mean learning to accept one another?
It's simply a question of sharing what we have
With another kind of being.[22]

The above quotation closes Remy Marion's informative and enjoyable book *On Being a Bear* He argues, "Contemporary human-bear relations are contrasting, if not paradoxical."[23] Countless children go to sleep hugging a teddy bear. Who hasn't heard the story of "Goldilocks and the Three Bears," or read the book or seen the film about Winnie-the-Pooh? Smokey the Bear is the mascot of the National Park Service's wildfire prevention program. I remember getting a good laugh when I heard Dale Marsen's "Waltzing with Bears" on public radio.

Ancient cultures revered the bear as our sibling—even as a human clothed in fur. Marion tells us, "When a dead bear is stripped of its skin, it can look uncannily like a human being."[24] Perhaps that is what prompted ancient hunters to think of bears in that way. Andrews notes, "The bear is a powerful symbol and image in both myth and lore. Stories abound of individuals turned into bears, bears into humans, and bears as gods."[25] Ursa Major (greater bear) is the most conspicuous constellation in the northern hemisphere. It contains the stars that form the Big Dipper.

Many cities are named for bears, including Bern, Switzerland. Russia, which has more bears than any other country, has the bear as its national animal. Longtime friends once lived in White Bear Lake, Minnesota. Bear Lake Road in Rocky Mountain National Park is the route to most of my favorite hiking trails in the park. I grew up rooting for the Chicago Bears and am a lifelong Chicago Cubs fan.

Maybe it was inevitable that an animal as large and powerful as the bear came to be feared, baited, hunted down, humiliated by bear trainers, and trapped in zoos. I pray that we can have a new understanding—really a restoration of the respect Native Americans have for the bear and its relation to us.

President Theodore Roosevelt experienced the paradoxical relationship while on a bear hunting trip in 1902. He refused to shoot a young bear that others in his hunting party had captured. He told them their behavior was unsportsmanlike. Newspapers picked up the story and illustrated it with cartoons of "Teddy" and the bear. A Brooklyn toy maker read the story and, with the permission of the president, created and sold the first stuffed teddy bears. Roosevelt promoted them as his re-election mascot. My guess is most of the children hugging their teddy bears when they go to sleep have never heard of the stuffed animal's origin.

I have two stories of bears—neither involving hunting! I served a congregation in a small town three hours north of the Twin Cities. During the summer months, the population increased greatly with campers, fishermen, and seasonal residents. Our second service was outside in a large area surrounded by trees. Folks stayed in their vehicles and listened to and participated in the service on car speakers. (The space had been a drive-in theater at one time.) I led the worshjp service from a tall A-frame.

At the back of the area was a space called Kids' Corner. During the sermon time, children would gather there with a Sunday school teacher. One Sunday, just as I was about to tell the children it was time to go there, I noticed two bear cubs sitting on the benches in Kids' Corner. I had to think quickly and tell a little lie: "Parents, the teacher isn't here today. *Please* keep your children in the car." Those two bear cubs stayed still on those benches throughout my sermon. Then they wandered off into the woods. What attracted them to that site with all those vehicles filled with people? Hundreds worshipped with us there every Sunday. Why did the bears stay and sit still to listen to my message? God only knows. Bears are curious creatures. They are attracted to new things, new smells, new experiences.

I had an amazing experience one summer day while hiking on a trail on the North Shore, near Lake Superior. I saw a stretch of raspberries just waiting to be picked. As I was munching on the delicious treat, a large black bear suddenly, silently appeared on the other side of the raspberry bushes. The bear showed wonderment but no aggression. Because I was not between a mama bear and her cubs, I felt no fear. I just was awed at being so close to a bear, one of the largest land mammals. I told the bear that I was sorry if I was eating its raspberry patch. I said it was an honor to meet it. Finally, the bear just shook his head and wandered back into the woods. I continued up the trail.

It was the most powerful reminder I had ever had of the truth that, when we show no aggression and no fear, then the creature we encounter does not either. Of course, there are some exceptions to this. Certainly, we need to show common sense. But I am concerned that we need to recover the God-intended relationship between humans and animals.

There is much we could say about bears as a powerful symbol. There are two characteristics of bears that can speak to us. First is the way bears travel. They take the same pathway year after year. Marion notes, "Using these well-worn trails to get from A to B helps them conserve energy, steer clear of humans, and move as stealthily as possible."

We keep making the same mistakes if we do not learn from the past. If we learn from it, we can build on the past and make progress. One of my favorite passages of Scripture is from Hebrews: "Therefore, since we are surrounded by so great a cloud of witnesses, let us also lay aside every weight and the sin that clings so closely, and let us run with perseverance the race that is set before us" (12:1).

We do not need to do the new thing just for the sake of newness. Just as the bears travel the same path for good reasons, so there are good reasons for us to follow traditions. Traditions strengthen family ties across generations. Traditions help us define who we are. We follow traditions not because we have to, but because they can help us on our life's journey. We should not follow traditions blindly. They need not bind us to the past, but they can help us conserve energy and steer clear of danger.

I remember well when some Sunday school teachers and their spouses came to my annual smorgasbord for groups in the congregation.

Some got tears in their eyes because they recognized the smells of traditional foods—foods they no longer prepared. Now I eat those traditional foods only occasionally. When I do, I think of my Swedish grandmother, a woman of great grit, faith, courage, and love. She helped shape me into the woman I am today. I also think of her two daughters, my aunts, who were also women of great grit, faith, courage, and love, and who encouraged me and showered me with love.

Remember that bears are attracted to new things. They check them out. They are also quick to pick up on positive or negative reinforcement. We follow in the footsteps of others so that we have a solid basis on which to test new things, to make a new way before us.

If you live where bears live, you know they bulk up before hibernating. Bears have an awareness of when it is time to seek shelter. They do not so much hibernate as have a deep sleep in the winter months. The depth of their sleep depends on the fat stored. During this deep sleep, the female bear gives birth to her cubs.

As humans, we need to go to deep places inside ourselves, to meditate, to do intentional reflection, to get in touch with the Spirit within. That inner work can bring healing, new insight, a sense of oneness with the universe, and a renewed sense of God's constant presence in our lives. Because we all are different in personality and experiences, there is no one right way to go to a deep place within. It is also easier for some personality types to go there than others. Some set aside a special place in their home, light a candle, and sit silently. Some play soft music. Some journal. Some of my deepest meditation times have come while weeding my garden, sitting at a lake, and hiking a mountain trail. The thing we need to do is experiment with what works best for us. Just as the bear knows when it is time to hunker down, so we need to heed signs when we need to go deep.

Many Native American and First Nation initiation rituals involve fasting and an extended period of isolation. The transition to adulthood is seen as a kind of rebirth, akin to the bear's emergence from a deep sleep. We go to deep places within so we can come out, renewed, re-energized to live lives filled with love for ourselves, for others near and far, and for God.

For Reflection:

1. As a child, did you sleep with a stuffed animal, a doll, or a pet? How did that affect you?
2. Who helped shape you?
3. Are there family traditions you still keep? Why or why not?
4. What are some lessons you have learned from grandparents, aunts, and uncles?
5. How often do you take time for deep reflection and meditation?
6. How do these times impact you?

Chapter 7

Song Birds

No wild animal lives so freely and in such variety among humans as do birds.[26]

Jim Robbins

Each year, thousands of people take up the enjoyable hobby of bird watching or birding. They learn to identify the hundreds of species in their own region. Some go on to try to see all the species possible—about 10,000 in total. Some even make a competition out of how many species they can observe.

I have fed birds for decades. I learned to place feeders out of reach of squirrels. I enjoy watching the colorful creatures at the feeder from my patio window. I have seen how bird behavior seems to resemble human behavior in all its variety.

My feeder has six feeding stations. Sparrows will feed at all six, while some perch on a nearby branch waiting their turn. Chickadees come one at a time, fill their mouths, and go to a branch to eat their breakfast or dinner. Some birds are bullies and push others away. Some are more comfortable eating the sunflower chips that fall to the ground. Small birds flee when a large bird comes to feed.

Every spring, a male robin arrives early and eats the seeds that have fallen to the ground. On occasion, I have seen robins during the winter months. Perhaps, with global warming, more will stay all winter. Do you know that there is a common legend that the robin received its red breast when it pulled a thorn from the bloodied crown on Jesus's head as he hung on the cross?

I love seeing robins. But the bird I have grown most fond of is the chickadee. Chickadees are fearless. They will take on larger birds that threaten them. Yet they play well at the feeder. I had read one could get a chickadee to eat out of one's hand. I tried it. I sat still with my arm outstretched and sunflower chips in my hand. Chickadees perched on a nearby branch looking at me. By the third day, they were eating out of my hand. I was amazed at how little the chickadee weighed. Of course, it is its light weight that enables it to fly.

For the Cherokee Indians, the chickadee is the bird of truth. An old tale tells of a witch who terrorized the whole tribe. She would wait in hiding and then kill anyone who passed by. Because she was made mostly of stone, it was hard to stop her. One day, a fearless chickadee landed on her and showed the warriors where she was vulnerable to attack. Knowing the truth frees us. That is an important lesson to remember in a time when some doubt there are any truths, and some think what they believe is the truth in spite of evidence to the contrary.

When I go walking or hiking, I usually hear a bird singing before I see it. The authors of *animal kind* write this about bird songs.

> The bird songs we hear every day are more than Beautiful. They serve a practical purpose. Birds employ their voices to call their mates, find their flock, claim territory, scare off intruders, warn others about predators and countless other functions.[27]

About 4,500 or more species burst into song. One-fifth of these have five or more songs. The brown thrasher, found in New England and Canada, has the most: 3,000. Robbins notes that "Chickadee language—both calls and songs—is the most sophisticated language in the world; scientists have spent decades studying it."[28] Bird songs have inspired many composers. Beethoven and Mozart come to mind. Birds also call to me to let me know it is time to fill the feeder.

Over the centuries, people of many cultures have been enamored with birds. There has been a deep connection between native peoples and birds across time. Robbins notes, "In countless myths, [birds] transform into people and vice versa, and they have long been conflated with angels and with other mysterious beings and have been thought to have special powers." Many Native Americans see birds as "fellow travelers, sometimes as a kind of extended family."[29]

Most of us are aware of birds leaving our yards and parks when fall arrives. Only 1,800 of the world's 10,000 bird species migrates in the fall to warmer climates, where food is plentiful, and then return again to more temperate regions in the spring. The big question is: what will global warming mean for their migration patterns? Friends have commented that they are seeing fewer and fewer birds each year.

You may have heard of the proverbial canary in the coal mine. In the nineteenth century, coal miners in England and Wales, and later in the United States, carried a pair of caged canaries with them as safety equipment. If they saw one lying distressed or dead, they knew the carbon monoxide levels were too high for them and they fled the mine. Canaries were used in this way until the 1980s, when they were replaced by electronic equipment. We will never know how many of these beautiful birds gave their lives to save the lives of miners.

We need to become cognizant of who the proverbial canaries in the coal mine are for us today. Who makes you aware of the problems you and our country face? Remember the chickadee as the bird of truth. Who are the proverbial chickadees that make clear the truth we need for safety and progress, and for personal and interpersonal growth?

Sometimes fire, flood, wind, or drought force us to migrate. Sometimes we move for work or retirement. Sometimes we need to make a move but are stuck in a rut. As someone once said, a rut is a grave with the ends knocked out.

It reminds me of one of my favorite stories about Jesus. A crippled man is lying among many invalids near a pool of water that was believed to bring miraculous healing if one reached the water when it was "stirred up." The man is bitter because no one has helped him reach the healing water. Jesus walks up to the man and his first words are, "Do you want to be healed?" The man says no one has helped him. Jesus simply replies, "Stand up; take up your mat and walk" (John 5:1–5).

It may be easier to blame others for our ills; however, it is usually a lame excuse for our inaction. Remember what I wrote about difficulty in forgiving my brother. That was a stand up and walk moment. There may have been crippling experiences in our lives, but God does not want us to just stay in a rut of self-pity. We need to get up and do the hard work of healing—whatever it takes. The One who loves will give us a hand to help.

Scientists are discovering that sharing information in the flock is likely essential to the survival of the individual as well as the flock. When the number of birds in the flock falls, there is a loss of information because each individual carries its own unique knowledge based on experience. It is a fallacy to think anyone can make it on his or her own. We all have had people who have helped us, guided us, and encouraged us on our way.

The variety of birds that share my feeder also symbolize for me the need to accept and celebrate the growing diversity of people in our country. I have found cross-cultural experiences enjoyable, lively, and enriching. The focus needs to be on what we gain rather than what we think we may be losing.

Remember the brave little chickadee. We can be braver than we think we can. Robbins challenges us all:

> If we learn to move beyond the subconscious terror we all carry and the emotional numbing we take on to shield ourselves, if we can tap into the extraordinary power of the birds and bottle this lightning, if we learn from our relationship with birds to fully understand...the full range we are capable of feeling and sensing in the world, we will find something inexhaustible and profound, even life-changing.[30]

Reading his book, it becomes clear that Robbins has found it.

For Reflection:

1. Is there something you need to get rid of so you can fly toward your goals?

2. In the long months of staying home because of the COVID-19 pandemic, how did you keep healthy physically, emotionally, and spiritually?

3. Some of us are extroverts and some of us are introverts. Which are you? How does this affect your behavior in the flock?

4. What feeds you spiritually? If you are malnourished or hungry, where might you find food?

5. There is an old saying that a bird in the hand is worth two in the bush. What does this suggest to you? Does it suggest needed action or insight you have gained?

Chapter 8

Bald Eagle

For he will command his angels concerning you, to guard you in all your ways. On their wings they will lift you up so that you will not dash your foot upon a stone.

Psalm 91:10–11

Benjamin Franklin was clearly a wise man; however, I am glad that the other founders of our nation shot down his idea to make the wild turkey our national symbol. Anyone who has seen a flock of wild turkeys prancing in a yard or on a road understands the wild turkey does not cut it. The bald eagle, on the other hand, stirs our hearts when we see one soaring overhead. The eagle has been a symbol of power and courage since ancient times. Andrews notes, "Every society which has had contact with eagles has developed a mythology and/or mysticism about them."[31]

So imagine my surprise when I saw an eagle up close. While I served the congregation mentioned in the bear chapter, I lived in a lakeside parsonage. Whenever possible, I came home for lunch. One noon, as I looked out the large picture window, a bald eagle landed on the deck railing. It spread its wings, looked back at me for a few moments, and then flew downward toward the lake. The eagle then flew back to the deck railing and showed me the large fish it had caught. It was as if the bald eagle was showing off! Finally, it flew away to eat its lunch or feed its eaglets.

I stood there awed with one of my favorite hymns—"On Eagle's Wings"—playing in my mind. It was as if the eagle had given me a reminder of God's love and care for me. The congregation was dealing with growing pains, which added to my workload and my stress. I needed God's support for my ministry. That day I was given a reminder that God is always there for me, lifting me up when I fall.

Eagles are among the largest of birds. They weigh about as much as a bowling ball and have a wingspan of more than seven feet. They almost disappeared from the United States because of the widespread use of DDT. Our national symbol was down to 450 nesting pairs when it was put on the national endangered species list in 1967. Because DDT was banned and reintroduction programs started, bald eagles have recovered. There are now about 10,000 pairs. Habitat loss, and mercury and lead poisoning remain threats, but the banning of DDT shows what can be done for our animal companions.

Eagle parents can teach human parents a thing or two. First of all, they mate for life. Both father and mother share in the raising of their children. When it is time for the eaglets to leave the nest, their parents take them on their powerful wings and then drop them. If an eaglet is unable to fly on its own, the parent picks it up on its wing and repeats the process until the eaglet can fly on its own.

It may seem like tough love. Tough love makes tough kids, tough enough to pick themselves up whey they fall or fail. Kids need to learn from their mistakes. They need to develop their abilities and accept their limitations. They need to learn that choices have consequences. I remember my youngest brother, when he was a child, telling me that he didn't think our parents loved him because they didn't discipline him. Discipline, appropriate to the circumstance, is an act of love. It helps a child get ready to fly.

Before becoming a pastor, I spent thirteen years in university student personnel work. In my role as assistant dean, and then dean of women, I counseled many students. Most blamed their parents for their problems. Some felt their parents paid too little attention to them and some too much. Healing came only when a student accepted it was time to fly—to accept that she or he was responsible for his or her own action, reaction, or inaction. It was common for these students to tell me, sometimes months later, that they now knew they could do and be far more than they ever thought they could do or be. In other words, they could fly.

When we compare God's care to that of eagle parents, it is clear that flying solo is not what God intends for us. God is with us always, even when we are unable to sense God's presence. God knows we have ups and downs. Sometimes it feels as if all is well and we can soar like an eagle. Then something happens to shake our confidence. Someone betrays us. Someone we love dies. We lose our job. We have a health crisis. The stubborn Delta variant impedes progress toward an end to a long pandemic.

It is as if life is two steps forward and then one back. Progress is slow and difficult; however, we can stay hopeful. I firmly believe that with God's Spirit within us, enabling, empowering, and enlightening us, we will persevere. Love will triumph in the end. I firmly believe God loves us just as we are, but loves us too much to leave us there, short of our God-given potential.

Jesus taught us the power of sacrificial love. God's Spirit enables us to do more than we think we can do. With God's help, we can soar to new heights of love for God, self, and neighbors near and far. When we start to fall, God swoops in to pick us up.

If God seems absent, we need to ask: who moved? If we stubbornly think we can make it on our own, if we neglect time for prayer and meditation and worship, it is hard to be aware of God's presence. My faith has been strengthened by parishioners who shared that they felt closer to God in the darkest times of their lives. As they lamented the loss of a loved one through death or divorce, they felt God's love surrounding them, enabling them to make faltering steps forward.

Others could not feel God's presence but kept their faith in God's love and were upheld by the love of family and friends. As the father of a very ill son cried out to Jesus, "I believe; help my unbelief." We need to be honest with our doubts and fears. God certainly knows what they are and why we have them. I have long loved how Frederick Buechner defined doubt.

> Whether your faith is that there is a God or that there is not a God, if you don't have any doubts you are kidding yourself or asleep. Doubts are the ants in the pants of faith. They keep it awake and moving.[32]

Doubts can lead to a greater understanding and acceptance of the divine mystery, a deeper and more mature faith. That certainly has been my journey. As great as bald eagle parents are, they cannot compare with God's steadfast, awesome love.

For Reflection:

1. Have you ever seen a bald eagle soaring above you? If so, what was your reaction? If not, are there places you could go to see them?
2. When and where has God seemed close to you?
3. When God seemed far away, did you seek God in new ways?
4. If you are a parent, how does your parenting compare with the tough love shown by eagle parents?
5. In what ways have doubts been "ants in the pants of faith" for you? Where has that led you?

Chapter 9

Elk

The wolf shall live with the lamb, the leopard shall lie down with the kid, the calf and the lion and the fatling and a little child shall lead them.

Isaiah 11:6

The prophet Isaiah looks to a future time when wild and tame animals will live peacefully with humans. Clearly that is not how things are today. Tame or domesticated animals become pets or sources of food. Many are afraid of wild animals. Farmers and ranchers may shoot them to protect their crops and herds. Some hunters make a sport of killing wild animals to put trophies on their walls.

Signs in our national parks warn visitors to not approach wild animals. In and around Rocky Mountain National Park, elk are some of the most commonly seen wild animals. Elk are the largest land animals in America. They are powerful, imposing, and have great stamina.

One certainly would not want to walk up to a herd of elk. Imagine my surprise, then, when a herd of elk surrounded me. It had been a beautiful late fall day and I wanted to get in one last hike before the snow began to fall. Cub Lake Trail is a safe one in the park to hike alone. As I was coming down from the lake, I paused at a wide spot on the trail to look at the bright blue sky and express thanks for the privilege of living an hour from the park.

It was a shock to be suddenly surrounded by about a dozen elk—females and a few yearlings. When I was in the middle of them, it was clear how big they are. Yet they were not threatening.

They did not bump me. They gave me room to walk at their pace. I had to walk with them until they walked away from me. It was an encounter of a lifetime. A park ranger was very surprised when I told her what had happened.

When I got to my car that day, I sat for a while. I recalled Isaiah's words and his picture of a peaceful kingdom. I pondered if those elk had given me a snapshot of what life in heaven will be like. I certainly hope so.

Female elk weigh about 500 pounds and stand four to five feet at the shoulder. Prior to European settlement, more than ten million elk roamed over nearly all of the United States and Canada. By the late 1800s, they were wiped out in the eastern United States.

The Shawnee Indians named the animal *wapiti*. Whites gave it the name elk after a European relative which more closely resembles a moose. I saw a moose up close one day while hiking; the elk does not resemble the moose. Moose tend to live alone. Elk live in herds, staying mostly with their own gender—like many parishioners do at the coffee hour after worship.

In another awesome national Park—Grand Teton—I was sitting on a log by a shallow lake when a bull moose suddenly appeared. He looked at me, decided I was not a threat, and dropped back down into the shallow water. It was just another reminder that if we do not show fear or aggression, wild animals will most usually just take us in stride.

As I reflected more on what was a once-in-a-lifetime experience with that herd of elk, I realized that in the middle of that herd, I was walking more slowly than I usually walked. From the time I was a young child, I worked hard and played hard. I walked fast and read fast. It all made it possible for me to work full-time while working on my MA and PhD.

I know I am not the only one to work hard and fast. One can accomplish much that way. But we need to be aware of the limitations of such a lifestyle. I remember a parishioner who came to see me. He was a businessman who had worked hard to rise to the top of his field. He told me his wife was leaving him and he did not know why. "After all," he said, "I told her once that I loved her. Wasn't that enough? I provided well for her and the kids." That parishioner did not realize that what his wife and children wanted most was for him to be truly present to them. They wanted him to show interest in them and to demonstrate his love by his actions. Strengthening relationships takes time and attention and care.

It reminds me of another parishioner and what she said to me early in my ministry. She was a woman who knew how to tell the truth in a loving way. She told me that sometimes I did not seem to hear people and she knew the problem was not with my ears. The problem was my overactive brain. Because of her, as part of my getting ready in the morning, I told myself, "Barb, remember to focus on the person before you and actively listen!" That routine helped me to slow down and truly listen—at least most of the time.

Slowing down is necessary to foster better, fuller relationships with family, friends, and colleagues. When we spend time together, we strengthen bonds by playing and praying together, laughing and crying together, and serving together.

Even so, for some of us hard chargers, we need reminders from others to slow down. As the old saying goes, all work and no play makes a dull person. God wants us to experience life-giving relationships. God wants us to work and play, serve and pray, laugh and love. God wants us to be in a relationship with animals—to care for them, to share space with them, to celebrate their beauty and respect their power. I thank God for the elk who reminded me of that.

For Reflection:

1. Have you ever joined a group of persons unlike you in some ways? What was that like for you?

2. Think of the relationships you have had with family, friends, and colleagues. What have you done to strengthen those relationships? Have some relationships withered from lack of attention?

3. Is it hard for you to slow down? What helps or hinders you?

4. Is there someone you need to speak the truth in love to—for their sake and yours?

5. Why do you think we call the animals "elk" instead of "wapiti"?

Chapter 10

Butterflies

Let us take pleasure in colorful butterflies; let us admire the funny interactions among these little creatures and be thankful that insects work on our behalf.

Anne Sverdrup-Thygeson[33]

M any folks have found pleasure in watching butterflies dancing from flower to flower. For me, it has been an enjoyable break from weeding in my garden or flower beds. Butterfly conservancies are popular tourist destinations. The overwintering habits of the monarch butterflies in Mexico draw tourists from around the world. My focus is on the monarch butterfly. This beautiful insect has symbolized transformation and metamorphosis for so many cultures. I have had two memorable experiences with these colorful creatures.

The first experience came at a decision-making point in my life. I had made lists on a yellow pad of the pros and possible cons of the two choices before me. Then, one early morning, I hiked to a favorite mountain lake and sat with the pad in my lap. After a short time in prayer, a monarch butterfly landed squarely on one of the choices. It stayed there for several minutes. From the distance of time, I can see that choice was the direction God intended me to take. A monarch butterfly flittered along side of me until I reached my car. Another one greeted me when I arrived home. It was as if God was using monarch butterflies to make sure I received the message. It also seemed a display of God's sense of humor.

I am even more thankful and amazed by the second encounter. One day, a young couple called me. We had never met but they asked me to come to the cemetery south of town for a burial service.

They and a few family members and friends would be there for the burial of the couple's child, who had lived for only two days. As I drove to the cemetery, I prayed that I could be a source of comfort and give hope to the grieving couple.

We spent some time together getting acquainted. I read some scripture and prayed. As the father, with his large hands holding the small coffin, started to place it in the ground, a large monarch butterfly appeared. It circled the coffin three times and then flew off. Amidst the tears of all there, I said, "God has given you a clear reminder that death is not the end. You will be reunited with your child some day in the future— for eternity." What an answer to prayer!

The monarch butterfly is seen at Easter time as a symbol of the resurrection of Jesus and the resurrection of all of God's children in the age to come. The word *resurrection* comes from the Latin word to rise from the dead. In Greek, it is *anastasis,* which means standing again or rising again. Both Latin and Greek imply a rebirth.

I believe we lose out when we think of resurrection only as something that comes after our death. God wants us to experience life fully in the here and now as well as in the age to come. On the other hand, we lose out if we ignore the gift of eternal life. Paul's words in First Corinthians are often read at burial services:

> *When this perishable body puts on*
> *imperishability, and this mortal*
> *body puts on immortality, then the*
> *saying that is written will be*
> *fulfilled: "Death is swallowed up in*
> *victory."*

> *1 Corinthians 15:54*

We can compare the life we live to the metamorphosis of the monarch butterfly. After mating, the female lays her eggs on a milkweed plant. After the caterpillar hatches from the egg, it spends two weeks consuming the plant. It then attaches itself to a stem of a leaf and spins itself into a chrysalis. About ten days later, a beautiful monarch butterfly emerges.

As the caterpillar consumes the milkweed plant, so we live in a consumer economy. It can lead us to focus only on our own wants and needs. It leads to the self-centering that is all too common these days. Consumerism says the one who has the most, the latest, and the best wins. The best-looking and the wealthiest are looked up to. Many find this a shallow, unsatisfactory way to live. Consumerism leads some to suffer anxiety and depression. Often, one needs to hit bottom before significant change can occur.

The apostle Paul, whose life was dramatically changed by an encounter with Christ, urges us:

Do not be conformed to the world
but be transformed by the renewal
of your minds, so that you may

discern the will of God—what is
good and acceptable and perfect.

Romans 12:2

Notice Paul writes, "be transformed," not transform yourself.

When the caterpillar spins itself into a chrysalis, its work is done. The caterpillar has within itself the substance needed for metamorphosis to happen, which it does during the ten days of rest.

Like the caterpillar, we need to rest and wait for new life to happen. Some go on a quiet retreat. Sitting in silence in nature is my favorite spot. A friend had a special place in her home. Some quietly meditate while others read Scripture devotionally. God urges us, "Be still and know that I am God" (Psalm 46:10). Many are shaped and nurtured in Christian community. I encourage you to discover what chrysalis space works best for you.

Remember, we are only ready for the chrysalis stage when we realize the need for it. Moreover, metamorphosis can come only when we go through the chrysalis stage. We cannot go around it to new birth. The chrysalis stage is where the Spirit of God transforms us.

I cherish a numbered print of a painting by Annie Seahorse Reagan that hangs in my living room. It portrays a Native American woman being transformed into a monarch butterfly. The title of the painting is *Empathy*. Empathy is the experiencing as one's own, the feelings of others.

Love is what prompts us to show empathy. Love enlivens and deepens relationships. Love is the glue that holds relationships together. Love is the essence of new birth. Paul called love the greatest spiritual gift.

When the monarch butterfly emerges from the chrysalis, it is a colorful, joyful thing to see as it flits from flower to flower. It is not weighed down by self-centered care. It shows no resemblance to a caterpillar. Transformation—metamorphosis—is complete.

Our transformation will be complete when this physical body becomes a spiritual body in the resurrection to come. But we can experience transformation in this life as well. We can lead lives of love. We can build others up rather than knocking them down. We can share our resources of time, money, and abilities to help those in need. In short, we can love others as God loves us.

Still, we kid ourselves if we think this is easy. This world is full of temptations. Humans seem bent toward self-interest. I have found going through the caterpillar—chrysalis—butterfly stages a repeated process that has led to greater love for God and others, and to a deeper appreciation for the divine mystery and the interconnectedness of all creation.

For Reflection:

1. Have you ever experienced an animal appearing to give you comfort or direction?
2. What stage are you in: caterpillar, chrysalis, or butterfly?
3. What would be the impact in the world if love became the dominant force?
4. What is more important to you: new life in the here and now, or new life after death?
5. Monarch butterflies are threatened as a species due to loss of habitat and pesticides. What might you do to help them?

Acknowledgements

LINDA FRENCH [ILLUSTRATOR]

After 32 years of teaching special needs students as well as raisin g a family, Linda found her passionate talent in painting animals. She trained Guide Dogs, Therapy Dogs, and currently volunteers for a dog rescue organization along with adopting abused dogs. Her pet portrait business incorporates the spirit and beauty of the animals she encounters. They can be viewed at Lindafrenchart.com.

Epilogue

The nine animals I encountered, ranging from monarch butterfly to bear, and from spider to a herd of elk, are not all my encounters; however, they are the most memorable. It is not likely that my experiences will be your experiences. However, we can all have meaningful encounters. All the animals we meet, whether we take the initiative, have a chance meeting, or the animals take the initiative, can change our perspective and our actions if we take the time to ponder the meaning of the encounter.

Two main themes underlie what I wrote and what you have read. First is the importance of relationships. We are created to be in relationship with God and with our fellow creatures, human and animal. Strengthening relationships takes time and attention. Saving or restoring relationships takes forgiveness. Being in relationship with animals takes being in their environment and seeing them in new ways as fellow creatures.

Second, I encourage doing what is needed for personal and spiritual growth as prompted by what the animal taught us. Regardless of our age, we can all grow in love, in word and deed. We have the tools to do that. It is a question of the will to do that. Cultural historian Thomas Barry offers these words of hope.

> We cannot doubt that we...have been given the intellectual vision, the spiritual insight, and even the physical resources we need for carrying out the transition that is demanded of these times, transition from the period when humans were a disruptive force on the planet Earth to the period when humans became present to the planet in a manner that is mutually enhancing.[34]

In that spirit, I am sharing some suggestions for caring for animal companions who share our planet.

1. Contact your local animal shelter or humane society. Learn what is needed. Volunteer your time. Adopt an animal there.

2. If you have the space, provide a habitat for birds, bees, and butterflies in your yard or on your patio. Plant flowers, shrubs, and trees that benefit them. See the National Wildlife Federation website for suggestions and help.

3. Donate to reputable organizations that are scientifically based and help animals thrive. The World Wildlife Fund and the Nature Conservancy are in my will, and I contribute regularly to the National Wildlife Federation, Audubon, and my local humane society.

4. There is increasing concern about the number of animals facing possible

extinction. Habitat loss and pesticide use are factors. But the greatest threat is global warming. Educate yourself on ways you can make a positive difference. We all need to do what we can.

5. If you want to learn more about the animals featured in this book, check out the books listed in the bibliography. You may find them in your public library.

Finally, thank you for reading this book. If you would like to contact me, e-mail me at bararalinder25@gmail.com.

Bibliography

Andrews, Ted. *Animal Speak*. Woodbury, MN: Llewellyn Publications, 2021.

Berry, Thomas. *The Great Work: Our Way into The Future*. New York: River Press, 1999.

Culin,Joseph. "Spider." Britannica.com. Last updated September 22, 2021. https://www.britannica.com/animal/spider-arachnid/additional-info#history.

Childs, Craig. *The Animal Dialogues*. New York: Back Bay Books, 2007.

Dillard, Annie. *Pilgrim at Tinker Creek*. New York: Harper & Row, 1985.

Doyle, Brenden. *Meditations with Julian of Norwich*. Santa Fe: Bear & Company, 1983.

Haupt, Lyanda Lynn. *Rooted: Life at the Crossroads of Science, Nature,*

and Spirit. New York: Little, Brown
Spark: 2021.

Kolbert, Elizabeth. "Where Have All the Insects Gone?" *National Geographic* (May 2020): pp.41-65._.

Louv, Richard. *Our Wild Calling*. Chapel Hill: Algonquin Books, 2020.

Marion, Remy. *On Being a Bear*. Vancouver: Greystone Books, 2021.

Newkirk, Ingrid, and Gene Stone. *Animalkind*. New York: Simon & Schuster, 2021.

Nicolon, Thomas. "Bites That Kill." *National Geographic* (June 2020): _pp. 128-161._.

Robbins, Jim. *The Wonder of Birds*. New York: Spiegel & Grau, 2017.

Svwedrup-Thygeson, Anne. *Extraordinary Insects*. New York: Simon & Shuster, 2019.

Tong, Wenfei. *Understanding Bird Behavior*. Princeton: Princeton University Press, 2020.

Whipple, A.B.C. *Critters*. New York: St. Martin's Press, 1994.

Wohlleben, Peter. *The Inner Life of Animals*. Vancouver: Greystone Books, 2017.

Notes

[1] Thomas Merton, *New Seeds of Contemplation*, (New York: New Direction Books, 1962), 130.

[2] Lyanda Lynn Haupt, *Rooted: Life at the Crossroads of Science, Nature, and Spirit,* (New York: Little, Brown Spark, 2021), 13–14.

[3] Richard Louv, *Our Wild Calling*, (Chapel Hill: Algonquin Books, 2020), 23.

[4] Ingrid Newkirk and Gene Stone, *animalkind,* (New York: Simon and Schuster, 2021), 4.

[5] St. Francis of Assisi, "The Canticle of Creatures," (Assisi: Minerva Editrice, 1992).

[6] Louv, *Our Wild Calling*, 28.

[7] Ted Andrews, *Animal Speak*, (Woodbury, MN: Llewellyn Publications, 2021), 265.

[8] Andrews, *Animal Speak*, 265.

[9] Louv, *Our Wild Calling*, 265.

[10] Louv, *Our Wild Calling*, 240.

[11] Louv, *Our Wild Calling*, 240.

[12] Annie Dillard, *Pilgrim at Tinker Creek*, (New York: Harper & Row, 1985), 177.

[13] Andrews, *Animal Speak*, 360.

[14] Amy Klobuchar, *Antitrust*, (New York: Alfred A. Knopf, 2021), 177.

[15] A.B.C. Whipple, *Critters*, (New York: St. Martin's Press, 1994), 41.

[16] Whipple, *Critters*, 43.

[17] Sir Walter Scott, *Marmion: A Tale of Flodden Field*, Canto 6, Stanza 17,

https://www.gutenberg.org/files/4010/4010-h/4010-h.htm.

[18] Anne Sverdrup-Thygeson, *Extraordinary Insects*, (New York: Simon & Schuster, 2019), 63.

[19] In *The New Book of Christian Quotations*, compiled by Tony Castle, (New York: Crossroad Publishing Company, 1989), 89.

[20] Andrews, *Animal Speak*, 330.

[21] Brendon Doyle, *Meditations of Julian of Norwich,* (Santa Fe: Bear and Company, 1983), 120.

[22] Remy Marion, *On Being a Bear*, (Vancouver: Greystone Books, 2021), 200.

[23] Marion, *On Being a Bear,* 178.

[24] Marion, *On Being a Bear,* 178.

[25] Andrews, *Animal Speak*, 250.

[26] Jim Robbins, *The Wonder of Birds*, (New York: Spiegel & Grau, 2017), xv.

[27] Andrews, *Animal Speak*, 126.

[28] Newkirk and Stone, *animalkind,* 55.

[29] Robbins, *The Wonder of Birds,* 180.

[30] Robbins, *The Wonder of Birds,* 285.

[31] Andrews, *Animal Speak*, 136.

[32] Frederick Buechner, *Wishful Thinking*, (New York: Harper & Row, 1979), 20.

[33] Sverdrup-Thygeson, *Extraordinary Insects,* 199.

[34] Thomas Berry, *The Great Work: Our Way into*

The Future, (New York: River Press, 1999),11.

www.ingramcontent.com/pod-product-compliance
Lightning Source LLC
Chambersburg PA
CBHW051653120626
46551CB00020B/1280